FASHION

FASHION

Lucia Mauro

VGM Career Horizons
a division of NTC Publishing Group
Lincolnwood, Illinois USA

Photo Credits:
Pages 1, 15, 29, 57, and 71: Fashion Institute of Technology/John Senzer; page 43: Photo Network, Tustin, CA. All other photographs courtesy of the author.

Library of Congress Cataloging-in-Publication Data

Mauro, Lucia.
    Fashion / Lucia Mauro.
        p.   cm. — (VGM's career portraits)
    Includes index.
    Summary: Considers career possibilities for children who have an interest in fashion and design. Includes success stories and suggestions for finding out more.
    ISBN 0-8442-4363-9 (hardback)
        1. Costume design—Vocational guidance—Juvenile literature.
    2. Fashion—Vocational guidance—Juvenile literature. [1. Costume design—Vocational guidance. 2. Fashion—Vocational guidance.
    3. Vocational guidance.] I. Title. II. Series.
    TT507.M379 1995   95-18547
    746.9'2'023—dc20   CIP
                                                                     AC

Published by VGM Career Horizons, a division of NTC Publishing Group
4255 West Touhy Avenue
Lincolnwood (Chicago), Illinois 60646-1975, U.S.A.
© 1996 by NTC Publishing Group. All rights reserved.
No part of this book may be reproduced, stored in a retrieval system, or transmitted in any form or by any means, electronic, mechanical, photocopying, recording or otherwise, without the prior permission of NTC Publishing Group.
Manufactured in the United States of America.

5 6 7 8 9 0 QB 9 8 7 6 5 4 3 2 1

Contents

Isn't it grand! Isn't it fine! Look
    at the cut, the style, the line!
The suit of clothes is altogether, but
    altogether it's altogether
The most remarkable suit of clothes that
    I have ever seen.

Frank Loesser
"The King's New Clothes"
(From the film *Hans Christian Andersen*)

Dedication

To Mom, Dad, and Joe for their constant encouragement
and love.

Introduction

Ever wonder how those hip clothes or cool earrings you're wearing get from the drawing boards to your neighborhood store, before landing in your closet? Or what it takes to turn your favorite movie star into a memorable character through costume design? And what about all those fashion magazines that help you plan your wardrobe? They had to come from somewhere or someone. Think of how exciting it would be if you were a big player in the contemporary fashion scene.

This book is a key starting point if the ever-changing world of fashion intrigues you enough to pursue it as a career. Each chapter will tell you about the variety of job opportunities available in fashion. You'll even get to meet a diverse group of clothing designers, buyers, boutique owners, textile instructors, fashion journalists, and photographers who comprise this exciting profession. And you'll find out what happens on the job, the pros and cons of the industry, the rewards, the pay, the perks, and the education you'll need. But, most importantly, this book will help you determine if you have the skills and personality to succeed in fashion.

FASHION
DESIGNER

I f you've got a knack for setting trends, a career as a fashion designer might appeal to you. A combination of talent, timing, creativity, and great networking skills are often the ingredients for a successful career in this field. But don't let the glamour, celebrity, and high salaries cloud your vision. There are only so many Calvin Kleins and Donna Karans in this fiercely competitive industry. Most high-fashion designers are self-employed and design for individual clients, or cater to specialty and department stores.

What it's like to be a fashion designer

Your career will include many disciplines, including sketching, pattern-making, and sewing. And contrary to your typical image of the celebrity high-fashion designer, your job will most likely involve more manual labor than glitz. Because most designers work for themselves and do custom-tailored work, they put in long hours selecting fabrics, cutting patterns, and sewing. But your designs—regardless of where you work—have the power to determine the "line," color, and materials that will be worn each season.

Let's find out what happens on the job

Because fashion design is such a creative field, rarely are there set hours. You may have an idea for a fabulous suit in the middle of the day and find yourself working until midnight to get the cut, color, and styling just right. You also have to devote a lot of time marketing yourself to boutique owners and large apparel centers, where you think your designs would sell. And don't forget about promoting yourself each season at fashion shows and upscale parties. All of these activities require huge chunks of time. So it's often helpful for designers to have assistants and extra tailors, or seamstresses. If you're on the staff of a department store, expect to work regular 9-to-5 hours.

The pleasures and pressures of the job

The opportunity to influence fashion trends through your designs will give you a great sense of satisfaction. If you cater to high-end markets, you may even rub elbows with celebrities and earn a lot of money and fame, too. But, on the flip side, you must be prepared to accept rejection and constructive criticism. Your peers will also compete intensely with you in an industry that's filled with mega-egos. Deadlines and social obligations will add to the pressure, as well as the constant strain of having to invent a new look or style.

The rewards, the pay, and the perks

Designing clothes is like creative art that people happen to wear on their backs. So it's very rewarding to know that you've contributed to an individual's sense of style. Of the approximately 300,000 designers in the United States, one-third are self-employed. Therefore, salaries vary depending on market swings and how popular your designs are. Generally, average weekly earnings of experienced full-time designers are $585. Employment in fashion design is expected to grow through the year 2005. Besides the benefits that accompany any high-profile job, as a designer you'll get to travel, make your own hours, and be independent.

Getting started

No formal degrees are required to succeed as a fashion designer. Many begin by doing apprenticeships or working in retail. But taking classes at an accredited design school would certainly increase your knowledge of textiles, fabrics, ornamentation, and trends. College programs in fine arts exist throughout the United States. Professional schools also award certificates or associate degrees in design. Graduates of two-year programs generally qualify as assistants to designers. An ideal liberal arts background would include courses in art history, sketching, garment construction, and textiles. It's a good idea to start an eye-catching portfolio—a collection of your best design sketches—to prepare yourself for job interviews.

Climbing the career ladder

- Join a fashion association, like Fashion Group.
- Become a designer's assistant.
- Keep adding to your portfolio.
- Attend fashion shows, boutique openings, and parties.
- Take specialized courses at a local design school.
- Shop around for stores that fit your design style.
- Meet with fashion directors of major department stores.

- Learn "fashion speak."
- Send news releases to the fashion press.
- Keep abreast of trends via the Internet.
- Learn everything about the "biz," from designing to selling.

Now decide if fashion design is right for you

Designers' personalities are as diverse as the clothes they create and the models who wear them. Let's take a look at the latest trends in character traits that would make you a successful designer:

- Boundlessly creative
- Bold
- Meticulous
- Patient
- Open-minded
- Competitive
- Hard-working
- Energetic

Things you can do to get a head start

Here are some ways you can prepare for a career in fashion design:

- Take home economics or textile-related classes in high school.
- Work part-time at a boutique or fabric store.
- Keep a file of designs you've cut out of fashion magazines.
- Set aside time to sketch your ideas.

ℒet's ℳeet...

ℳaria ℛodriguez
ℱashion ℒesigner

In 1979, Maria began by weaving scarves and shawls on her hand loom. Today she heads her own high-quality fashion design company. Maria was chosen "Designer of the Year" by the Apparel Industry Foundation.

What first attracted you to a career in fashion design?

I believe my longtime interest in arts and crafts naturally inspired me to become a designer. Weaving fabrics intrigued me, and I basically taught myself how to sew. I started out making jackets from the scarves and shawls that I wove by hand. After I sold them to local boutiques, I was inspired to design a collection—which turned into full-time work.

Did you need any special schooling or training?

Because I'm self-taught, I can't say that formalized design training is for everyone. Through my hands-on experience working with different fabrics, I learned, for example, how to blend rayon, silk, and cotton for low maintenance and comfort. But I strongly recommend that young designers take basic business courses if they plan on starting their own company. My ten years' experience in accounts payable helped me tremendously.

What new challenges face up-and-coming designers?

Customers are spending less money on their wardrobes. Trendy clothes are no longer the way to go. Consumers are buying clothes that will last a very long time. So it's up to designers to provide them with durable, timeless styles that they can mix-and-match and wear in different seasons. Future designers should take courses in computer drawing in order to keep abreast of our industry's increasingly high-tech advancements.

What special skills do you need to be a good fashion designer?

You need to believe in your work and promote yourself. Another way to remain competitive is to specialize in a certain sector of clothing design, such as outerwear, sweaters made of organically grown cotton, or evening apparel. During the summer, my company apprentices several high school and college students who are interested in furthering their knowledge of the design industry.

What do you like most/least about your job?

The few drawbacks of my job include the long hours, handling shifts in buying habits, and rushing to fill late orders. But I couldn't imagine working in any other industry. The pros certainly outweigh the cons:

- Each day is different and exciting.
- I feel very free and independent.
- I take great satisfaction in creating clothes that people love.

A Day in Maria's Life

Although each day holds new surprises for Maria, her basic schedule goes something like this:

She arrives at her studio/production facility at 7:30 A.M.

First, she checks her messages and organizes her schedule for the day.

Then around 8 A.M., she brainstorms about fabrics for knits and examines color swatches with her assistant.

For the rest of the morning, she does preliminary sketches for her upcoming collection. In the garment industry, the pressure is always on because she works a year or more ahead of a particular season.

She tries to fit in a lunchbreak before sitting down at her loom and creating samples based on earlier sketches. The natural light that pours into her loft-studio shows the colors in their purest form.

Around 3 P.M., she meets with her national sales director who has just returned from promoting her line at the city's apparel mart.

If she's satisfied with the samples she has created, and she is caught up with her various appointments and messages, she closes up shop around 4 P.M. On busier days, she stays until 5 P.M. If she's working on a fashion show, she works into the evening.

Let's Meet...

Emo Pandelli
Fashion Designer

Emo designs and sells women's sportswear and evening attire. His seasonal clothing collections combine organic fibers with ultrafeminine fabrics. He loves to create "clothes with a purpose."

What first attracted you to a career in fashion design?

As a child in my native Argentina, I was always surrounded by fabrics and the inspiration to create lovely things. My aunt sewed such beautiful clothing that I, too, wanted to make very exquisite items to wear. I designed my first pair of pants when I was seven years old.

Did you need any special schooling or training?

Yes, even though I learned how to make clothes on my own. I didn't study fashion design immediately, because where I went to school—in Argentina and Switzerland—only a fine arts program was offered. But that was extremely helpful, because I learned how to spot high-quality fabrics and sharpened my artistic sense. When I came to the United States, I received more formalized design education and a business background that prepared me for a wholesale career.

What special skills do you need to be a good fashion designer?

You must really dedicate yourself to your work 100 percent. Don't be afraid to experiment with different fabrics or cuts. You learn through trial and error. Always remember that your goal is to make your customer look fabulous. Know all aspects of the business—from sketching, to cutting patterns, to marketing your designs.

Describe a happy moment on the job.

I have had so many. It's always a happy moment when a customer who is self-conscious about weight or another aspect of her body tries on one of my designs that makes her look attractive. Great clothes really boost a person's self-esteem. I meet many fascinating people, and we often become friends. Someone just stopped in to give me a bouquet of flowers. A gesture like that gives me inspiration.

What are the positive and negative sides to your job?

I'm most enthusiastic when I'm testing out unique fabrics and sketching ideas for new creations. Then I carry that energy into meeting with my customers, doing fashion shows, and scheduling out-of-town appointments with other industry professionals. I guess the only negative side is the hectic schedule.

Find Out Why Emo's Favorite Color Is Green

We've heard of Earth Day. But has the "green revolution" finally hit the world of fashion design? According to Emo, environmentally conscious clothing is the wave of the future. Here's what he's done to contribute:

He started a fashion line called "Green Life," which features stylish clothes made from organically grown cotton and recyclable materials. Believe it or not, a vinyl-type material is made from recycled plastic bottles, so you can look cool and help save the earth at the same time. Many of the natural fibers also help combat allergies.

Because fashion designers are becoming more conscious of the world's fragile environment, a brand new area is opening up to future designers in the garment industry.

You may want to take some time exploring the scientific side of fibers and certain materials that, when discarded, pollute the environment. Consider specializing in "green" clothing. It's one major step toward making the planet healthier while giving fashion a higher purpose.

Success Stories

Jil Sander

Jil Sander's elegant, sophisticated fashions have attracted the attention of celebrities, such as Barbra Streisand and Winona Ryder. Based in Hamburg, Germany, the designer has built a $200 million worldwide fashion and cosmetics empire that keeps growing. Her understated, classic women's clothes are a reaction to the opulence that most popular designers favor. Jil survived severe criticism of her first collection in Paris to become one of the most recognizable designers in the world.

Giorgio Armani

Discreet elegance best describes the enduring men's and women's fashions of Milan-based designer Giorgio Armani. When in 1975, at the age of 40, he created his first collection under his own name, Giorgio revolutionized the industry by removing the padding and lining from men's suits for a natural, unstructured look. He applied this same technique to womenswear, which turned into an even bigger success. His attention to superb tailoring has spawned a fashion empire that reports more than $762 million in annual sales. He's opened A/X Armani Exchange casual clothing outlets all over the world, while continuing to design his classic fashions.

Find Out More

You and fashion design

If you think you're fashion material, answer the following questions to see if you have what it takes:

- Are you an imaginative person?
- Do you like to draw?
- Are you a fashion-conscious dresser?
- Do you enjoy taking risks?
- Do you prefer to work independently?
- Are you competitive?
- Does travel appeal to you?
- Are you attracted to the fine arts?
- Do you like to work with fabric?
- Is sewing something you enjoy?
- Do you have an outgoing personality?
- Do you prefer to be challenged?

If you've answered "yes" to most of these questions, then you just may be cut out for a career as a fashion designer.

Find out more about becoming a fashion designer

For more information about careers in fashion design, contact the following organizations.

American Apparel Manufacturers
   Association
2500 Wilson Blvd.
Arlington, VA 22201

Clothing Manufacturers
   Association of the U.S.A.
1290 Avenue of the Americas
New York, NY 10104

The Council of Fashion Designers
   of America
1412 Broadway
New York, NY 10022

Fashion Group International
9 Rockefeller Plaza
New York, NY 10022

International Association of
   Clothing Designers
240 Madison Ave.
New York, NY 10016

Men's Fashion Association of
   America
240 Madison Ave.
New York, NY 10016

National Association of Schools of
   Art and Design
11250 Roger Bacon Dr.
Suite 21
Reston, VA 22090

ACCESSORY

DESIGNER

The clothes we wear are just the basics of how we express ourselves. The finishing touches that complete an outfit are called accessories in the fashion business. They run the gamut of jewelry, hats, and scarves to belts, shoes, handbags, gloves, and hair clips. Accessory designers don't necessarily need to be well-versed in sewing or pattern cutting. Instead, their profession requires intricate, highly specialized hand-work—like soldering and gluing—and drawing talents.

15

But they, too, are typically self-employed and design for individual customers, or sell to boutiques and large apparel stores.

What it's like to be an accessory designer

As an accessory designer, your unique talents and craftsmanship will remain steadily in demand. While many of these items can be mass produced, there still exists a need for special, handmade things. In the endless field of jewelry, for instance, you may work for a large firm that uses your design talents for sketching and even building a ring, bracelet, or necklace. Or you may focus on a special ethnic or modern geometric style and sell your pieces as miniature works of art. If you can fashion leather for belts and purses, or make hats, there are opportunities for you to work from your home, at a specialty store, or for a major design company.

Let's find out what happens on the job

Like a fashion designer, you can't expect to work regular hours—unless you work on-site at a specific accessory firm. Because accessory design is not as competitive as clothing design, you won't be involved in grueling fashion show schedules and self-promotion at key parties. But you'll still be networking, mainly through industry trade shows, art fairs, and one-on-one meetings with store owners. On the job, you'll do tedious sketching, metalworking, and fabric styling depending upon what specific area you choose.

The pleasures and pressures of the job

Variety and flexibility are two of the best reasons for becoming an accessory designer. You can apply your skills in many areas, and several different working arrangements are available to suit your lifestyle. Think of yourself as an artist who's doing more than setting fashion trends. You're contributing items to a person's wardrobe that will probably last longer than his or her clothing. A diamond ring, for example, is a cherished heirloom that can be passed from generation to generation. But, like an artist, you'll have to face the challenge of getting and maintaining steady work. Your biggest pressure is creating appealing, high-quality accessories that fit the demands of the consumer market.

The rewards, the pay, and the perks

The personal satisfaction a talented accessory designer receives from creating precious articles often outweighs the limited financial rewards for beginners. But the potential to earn upward in the millions for unique, sought-after creations is also an incentive to pursue this career field. About one-third of the approximately 300,000 overall designers in the United States are self-employed. Salaries fluctuate greatly. Based on recent government figures, average weekly earnings of experienced full-time designers are nearly $600. And the field is projected to grow into the 21st century. You'll also move in exciting creative circles and be able to structure your own hours if you choose to be your own boss.

Getting started

You can take many different educational routes to become an accessory designer. A formal degree in fine arts is one. Apprenticeships with a master craftsperson or hands-on experience are other, more common, options. To have the best of both worlds, you can combine classes in metalworking or jewelry design, for example, with a related job. Most schools with programs in art and design award a degree in art as opposed to a specific accessory field. Courses, however, are available in particular disciplines, such as hat design or leather products.

Climbing the career ladder

- Sign up for fine arts courses at an art or design school.
- Work one-on-one with a master craftsperson.
- Research designs from different cultures at your local library.
- Take a textile class or workshop at a museum.
- Keep abreast of trends via the Internet.

- Tout your sketches and samples to local boutiques.
- Send news releases to the fashion press.
- Follow clothing trends that will complement your accessory designs.

Now decide if accessory design is right for you

Just like matching accessories to your outfits, your personality should fit the demands of this versatile field. How do you measure up to a career in accessory design? Are you . . .

- Artistically inclined?
- Creative?
- Precise?
- Eager to learn?
- Independent-minded?
- Curious?
- Technically oriented?
- Flexible?

If you display more than half of these traits, then accessory design may just be the career for you.

Things you can do to get a head start

These suggestions will help you prepare for a career in accessory design:

- Enroll in art and textile courses in high school.
- Subscribe to top fashion and accessory magazines.
- Work part-time at a museum gift shop or specialty store.

Let's Meet...

Victoria Adams Hamlett
Jewelry Designer

Victoria traces part of her heritage to the Cheyenne and Creek Indians. She has used Native American techniques in her designs for almost 30 years. Her "horse medicine" earrings symbolize Blackfeet dance sticks.

How did you get started in jewelry design?

My mother was a seamstress, and my father taught wood and metal shop. Instead of buying things, they created them. As a child, I designed jewelry for my small handmade dolls—and eventually for myself. By the time I was in high school, I was doing beaded work and sewing clothes, too. Rock 'n roll band members were among my first customers in the late 1960s.

Did you need any special schooling or training?

I spent a few years studying art, hand engraving, and metalsmithing at major universities and academies. For five years, I worked in a gold jewelry store and learned how to set fine gemstones, do custom jewelry, and repair antique pieces. A well-respected silversmith and goldsmith inspired me to do hand floral engraving in silver.

Do you use the knowledge/skills you learned in school and as an apprentice on the job?

I use them all—everything, from selecting materials, sewing, and simple mechanics to my drawing and ceramics classes. After leaving art school, I traveled around the world for two years and spent time in museums learning about different cultures. Those experiences provided me with a solid foundation for my jewelry designs.

Describe a typical day at work.

I have very few typical days. But if I'm especially centered on what I'm creating, I head to my studio at 9 A.M. and begin assembling parts for jewelry designs at my workbench. Until noon, I move between my computer to review shipping and stock data, and my engraving and beadwork tables. After lunch, I continue designing until 4 P.M. when I leave to take a walk and clear my mind. I usually fit in a few more hours of work until dinnertime.

What do you like most/least about your job?

I love the freedom. My work is not what I'd call a "job"—it's my life. I have only myself to answer to for my success or failure. No one can fire me, and I don't have to go through a typical hiring process. The only drawbacks are the large amount of time spent sitting indoors. When you work for yourself, you have to be very disciplined, and you rarely get weekends off.

Victoria's Advice to Aspiring Jewelry Designers

If you decide on a career in jewelry design, figure out what you love most about the field. It may take a few years, but don't give up.

Expose yourself to all the arts—furniture design, fine arts, painting, sculpture, art history, and life drawing. Learn all you can about craft work—ceramics, sewing, metal design, and engraving. All of these subjects will add to your own personal concept of design.

Take as many jewelry design–oriented classes as possible, with attention to business and computer courses if you plan to be self-employed.

And always be aware of up-and-coming trends and styles.

Let's Meet...

Zully Alvarado
Specialty Shoe Designer

Zully, a native of Ecuador, turned her own disability from polio into a career designing shoes and clothes for the disabled and hard to fit. Since 1989, she has been creating shoes that she hopes will raise the self-esteem of the physically challenged.

Is a career in shoe design something you always dreamed of?

My childhood dream had always been to be a fashion designer. I was also encouraged by my aunt, who taught me how to sew and crochet at a very early age. After I decided to put myself through school, I did alterations to help pay for the tuition. I became increasingly disturbed by the lack of style in the orthopedic shoes I was required to wear. So I decided to design fashionable specialty footwear.

Tell me how you got started in specialized shoe design.

Around 1982, I began suffering from postpolio syndrome; I needed frequent bed rest and stress reduction. I needed to be able to have control over the hours I worked. So I later started my own business, focusing on creating stylish shoes for disabled and hard-to-fit customers. My goal is to raise the confidence level of people with disabilities through nonoffensive fashions—especially their shoes, which typically pull an entire outfit together.

Did you need any special schooling or training?

I took classes in fashion design and worked intensively with a shoe crafter for one year to learn the trade. My degrees, however, are in speech pathology; audiology, rehabilitation and administration; and early childhood education. When I was learning English, I decided to master the subject so well that I could teach others with language difficulties. My work in rehabilitation has enabled me to understand the physiology and special needs of my customers.

What special skills do you need to be a good specialty shoe designer?

You have to be well-versed in different grades of leather, various dyes, and chemicals. A fashion design background helps you understand line, color, and texture. But you should also be familiar with the anatomy and alignment of the body. Volunteer at a rehabilitation facility for additional awareness. Be patient and learn to treat disabled customers naturally without hesitation or fear.

The Story of Zully's Red Shoes

While Zully was studying fashion design, she found that being around such talented, creative people was very energizing. But, at the same time, she wanted to solve the problems of society. So she looked at what her own needs were, and the answer was shoes. She always wanted red shoes, but couldn't get them because of the problems with her feet. After working 12 to 15 hours a day for one year with a shoecrafter, she was confident enough to make a pair of shoes. The first thing she did was make her red shoes. And that's what she wore for her first fashion show.

Her advice to young people is don't dwell on your problems. Pursue your dreams. Along the road, there are people willing to help you. Allow them to help you.

Success Stories

Jean Schlumberger

Transforming nature—its flowers, tropical sea life, and butterflies—into delicate pieces of jewelry was the inspration behind Jean Schlumberger. He studied art, but had no formal jewelry design training. His career began in Paris in the 1930s and culminated in New York, where he was the creative force behind Tiffany & Co. from 1955 until his death in 1987 at the age of 80. The Alsatian-born jewelry designer wanted his work to "look as if it were growing, uneven, at random, organic, in motion."

Angela Swedberg

Angela Swedberg has restored the lost art of American Indian beadwork and quillwork to accessory and historic clothing design. Resurrecting techniques that were developed hundreds of years ago, she sought out craftspeople who taught her the trade. Through trial and error, Angela perfected the intricate, ritual-based methods of combining hides, feathers, and multicolored beads for creating one-of-a-kind pieces. Once she makes a purse or belt, the self-taught designer doesn't repeat a pattern. Instead, she assembles the best natural materials to re-invent new styles for her wearable art. She creates her art at her rural home-studio in the Pacific Northwest.

James Ciccotti

By studying past trends and adapting them to contemporary lifestyles, James Ciccotti has attracted the attention of accessory companies around the world. He designs neckties, sunglasses, corrective eyewear, hats, scarves, handbags, shoes—and men's clothes, too. While studying fashion design in the United States 13 years ago, James was chosen to do a three-month apprenticeship in Milan. In such a short time, a number of influential fashion professionals noticed his classic yet innovative designs. So he stayed in Europe, and today is sent around the globe by major design firms.

Find Out More

Find out more about becoming an accessory designer

To find out more about accessory design, contact:

Fashion Group International
9 Rockefeller Plaza
New York, NY 10022

Jewelers of America
1185 Avenue of the Americas
New York, NY 10036

Gemological Institute of America
1660 Stewart St.
Santa Monica, CA 90404

Manufacturing Jewelers and
    Silversmiths of America
100 India St.
Providence, RI 02903

Shoe Service Institute of America
Educational Library
5024-R Campbell Blvd.
Baltimore, MD 21236-5974

BUSINESS
AND
ENTERTAINMENT

A career in fashion doesn't limit you to designing trendy clothes or accessories. The field is so far-reaching that just about any subject you're interested in can turn into a fashion-related occupation. In this chapter, you'll meet people who work in the business and entertainment sectors of fashion, including a buyer and a costume designer.

What it's like to be in fashion business & entertainment

If you become a buyer for a major department store or specialty shop, you'll be a key decision maker in determining what styles will be most popular. You'll need a solid knowledge of fabrics, buying patterns, and fashion trends, along with some general business savvy. If you choose costume design as a profession, expect to understand all aspects of stagecraft and clothing's history in order to design practical, authentic period attire.

Let's find out what happens on the job

You can look forward to working regular 9-to-5 hours, with additional time spent attending merchandising shows around the world. If you're a buyer or sales representative, for instance, you'll have daily office hours filled with appointments with designers and store managers.

In the creative world of costume design, your hours will be less predictable. Like a high-fashion designer, you'll spend a lot of time sketching, cutting out patterns, and sewing, and you'll also attend rehearsals.

The pleasures and pressures of the job

BUSINESS

Pros: Steady work
Vast opportunity for growth
High salaries
Chance to travel
Major decision-making power

Cons: Heavy competition
Pressure-filled
responsibilities
Demanding bosses
Extensive business trips

ENTERTAINMENT

Pros: Creativity
Celebrity recognition
Chance to work with
well-known actors
No routine days
Highly specialized field

Cons: Limited job availability
Unpredictable hours
Low entry-level salaries
Temperamental
personality clashes

The rewards, the pay, and the perks

Salaries in most business-related positions are based on commission, especially for buyers and sales representatives. Apparel showroom reps receive salary plus commission, and often start at an annual salary in the high twenties. Because costume designers are so specialized, they have fewer career opportunities open to them. If they're employed by a major ballet, opera, or theatrical company, they would start at a salary in the mid to high teens, with the possibility of escalating to the high thirties or forties. But there are many intangible rewards such as artistic achievement and recognition.

Getting started

Ideally, to pursue a business fashion career, you should hold a bachelor's degree in marketing, sales, or communication, as well as a minor in textile design. Part-time work in a boutique or department store would be very helpful, too. Degrees in costume design are vast and varied. You might also consider volunteering with an area performing troupe, to get started in your career.

Climbing the career ladder

Here are some suggestions to point you in the right direction.

BUSINESS

- Take a textiles course.
- Get a job in retail.
- Do an independent research project tracking buying patterns of a particular store.
- Apply for an internship at your city's apparel center.

ENTERTAINMENT

- Attend local theatrical productions.
- Help design costumes for your school's plays.
- Take basic sewing and design courses.
- Visit museums and libraries to research period costumes.

Now decide if the areas of fashion business or entertainment are for you

Check the following list to see if you have what it takes to succeed in fashion's business or entertainment arenas.

BUSINESS

- Assertive
- Competitive
- Trendsetter
- Confident
- Stylish
- Mature

ENTERTAINMENT

- Innovative
- Flashy
- Driven
- Knowledgeable
- Personable
- Flexible

Things you can do to get a head start

In business, talk to people who work in the industry, and visit stores to study fashion trends. Read magazines to find out about the latest changes in styles. On the entertainment side, look at theater and film in a whole new way. Observe how costumes relate to the work, the quick backstage changes, and the ease with which they move for the performers' maximum comfort.

Let's Meet...

Lisa Petronaci
Fashion Sales Representative

Lisa has been a successful sales representative in the apparel industry for almost 10 years. She is addicted to the business' frenetic pace and competitive nature.

How did you know you would enjoy working as a sales representative?

I love working with people more than anything else. So I figured that the fashion world is filled with so many eccentric, creative people bursting with energy, I would automatically enjoy it. And it's really a blast!

Do you use the knowledge/skills you learned in school on the job?

Yes, but in a practical way. I received a bachelor of science degree, but most fashion students complete a 2-year program. Because I studied textile design, I often go back to my textbooks to brush up on design trends and fabric construction; that's part of my job of selling. Remember that what you learn in college is important, but how you use that knowledge to make yourself marketable is more important.

What special skills do you need to be a good sales rep?

Foresight. You absolutely have to be on top of what's going on. If you're not, you'll never survive. The industry moves very fast, and you have to keep up.

Is there a lot of competition for jobs in fashion sales?

There's too much competition across the board. Therefore, you need to know everything about the business and be completely honest with prospective employers. If you take a casual approach, know that there are about 50 people waiting to take your job. That's the reality of this business.

What do you see yourself doing five years from now?

Consulting within the industry and helping manufacturers to source their materials and become more profitable.

What advice would you give young people starting out in a fashion sales career?

Be prepared. Competition is the toughest it's ever been, so be constantly aware of what's going on in the field. Fashion is not as glamorous as it appears. In fact, it can be a downright dirty business, with your peers going to great extremes to get ahead. It's your job to outsmart them with your knowledge and business savvy.

Lisa's First Day on the Job

Of course, Lisa was scared, not knowing what to expect on her first day working as a sales representative for a major apparel center. Nevertheless, she hid her nervousness and learned as much as she could about the textile line she was assigned to sell.

No sooner had she started understanding the product, by afternoon, an important out-of-state customer walked in. The customer had originally scheduled an appointment with another sales assistant who happened to be out that day.

So Lisa was thrown in, and did the best she could to sell that textile line. And she sold it! She made mistakes, but the customer and Lisa had fun learning together. That gave her confidence for all her future sales opportunities.

Let's Meet...

Warren Pepperdine
Costume Designer

For the past 30 years, Warren has designed costumes for semiprofessional theatrical productions, and has taught theater arts and fashion on the university level. He's particularly fascinated with the styles of the 18th century.

Tell me how you got started in costume design?

I was a music and theater major in college, and my education included costuming. I started to do everything from drafting, to cutting, and sewing. I continued to design costumes while receiving my Ph.D. in directing and acting. Then I eventually made it a full-time career, which allowed me to utilize my broad theatrical knowledge and experience.

Did you need any special schooling or training?

Yes. Besides the advanced degrees in theater, I needed to learn about fabrics throughout history to make my costumes very authentic. That included knowing how people moved and sat in their clothes, as well as what type of architecture surrounded them. I spent a lot of time going to museums.

Describe your work environment.

Like most fashion designers, I work in a spacious studio where I sketch my ideas on large sheets of paper, before cutting out a pattern. I'm surrounded by dress forms and plenty of scraps of material and trims that I purchase at garage sales, flea markets, or thrift shops. I also spend a lot of time with the director of a production, and sit in on rehearsals.

What do you like most/least about your job?

The best part involves the excitement about creating the look of a show. You're working with set designers, actors, and directors— who are all equally creative and energetic. The downside of costume design is the long hours spent at rehearsals, fittings, finding the materials, and making the costumes. There are very few job openings available, and the pay scale is quite low. Performers can be temperamental, too.

What advice would you give young people starting out in costume design?

Don't expect to go to New York and design costumes for Broadway shows right away. You have to get in through the back door by volunteering to help local theaters with their set and costume construction. A great way to network is by assisting as a back-stage dresser, helping the actors get in and out of their costumes. And always keep in mind that you're designing clothes that must be seen from a great distance by an audience.

Warren's Favorite Costume Designs

- Warren designed a 35-foot, silver "peacock-style" train, with an equally flamboyant headdress, for a production of "Elektra." The actors also wore elaborately painted masks showing the play's shifting moods.

- Warren build wires and lightbulbs into a costume that lit up when the performer flipped a hidden switch.

- A version of Shakespeare's "As You Like It" was set in the Louisiana swamps, so Warren devised some intricate pairings of fishnet and Spanish moss.

- For a children's play set in the Middle Ages, Warren created multi-colored side-split, slip-over panels made of felt, featuring a variety of animals mirroring a "coat of arts" imagery.

Success Stories

John Rezny

Since 1989, John Rezny has been a buyer for a major U.S. furrier. Unlike buying standard clothing items, the fur industry involves a risky, highly expensive commodity. So he spent many years learning the craftsmanship and value of the pelts (or individual hides). Today he divides his busy schedule among fur auctions, trade shows, buyers' markets, and working the showroom floor. His knowledge ranges from polished sales techniques to how furs are made, styled, treated, and repaired.

Cathy Smith

Specializing in western-style fashions, Cathy Smith designs costumes for film and television. The Emmy Award–winning designer has worked on the costumes for Steven Seagal movies, as well as the TV miniseries, "Son of the Morning Star." Her infantry frock coat for the latter show is an exact replica of the ones worn during the Battle of Little Big Horn. Known for her work's authenticity, Cathy was trained by one of the last Sioux Indian elders in the sacred art of porcupine quillwork.

Find Out More

Reasons for choosing a career in the business or entertainment sides of fashion

Look over the following reasons individuals have chosen to pursue careers in fashion business or entertainment. If you agree with most of these statements, you should seriously consider preparing for either one of these occupations.

BUSINESS

- I like to be challenged on a daily basis.
- Only a superfast-paced career suits me.
- I enjoy meeting people.
- It's important for me to be part of a team.
- I can predict fashion trends.
- I'm not easily intimidated or discouraged.

ENTERTAINMENT

- The entertainment world intrigues me.
- I can be as creative as I want to be.
- I know a lot about fabrics and trims.
- I like working with actors and directors.
- I'm familiar with both stagecraft and clothing design.

- Long hours and deadline pressures don't wear me out.

Find out more about a fashion business or entertainment career

For additional information on the business and entertainment aspects of the fashion industry, contact these organizations.

Fashion Group International
9 Rockefeller Plaza
New York, 10022

Fashion Institute of Technology
Seventh Avenue at 27th Street
New York, NY 10001–5992

Manufacturers' Agents National
    Association
23016 Mill Creek Rd.
P.O. Box 3467
Laguna Hills, CA 92654

RETAIL
AND
PROMOTION

A fter an outfit is designed and made, it reaches the consumer through stores and extensive public relations efforts. While many fashion designers sell their products to department or specialty stores, at least one-third of the 300,000 professional designers in the United States own their own boutiques. And, if they want to get the word out to millions of prospective buyers, they need to work with a publicist, or promotional specialist.

What it's like to be a store owner or publicist

If you have an entrepreneurial spirit and good fashion sense, owning a boutique could be perfect for you. Freedom to purchase and sell designs you believe will turn heads is especially satisfying. You'll need money management skills to run a business, and stamina to work 7 days a week. As a fashion publicist, you'll meet with designers and other professionals to coordinate promotions. You'll do a lot of writing, travel frequently, and address large groups of people.

Let's find out what happens on the job

As a boutique owner, you must make critical decisions on a daily basis. You're totally responsible for your financial security. You'll hold meetings with designers whose work you're certain will sell, and you'll need to update the store's decor continuously so that it's eye-catching and inviting. In promoting your store, you need a public relations specialist to handle the media, news releases, the fashion press, and special events.

The pleasures and pressures of the job

Independence is one of the most attractive things about owning a store, and it can be both fun and challenging. In addition to meeting new people, you are a highly visible trendsetting force. On the downside, you must dedicate a good part of your life to the business. In the field of public relations, you'll encounter many exciting fashion leaders. The travel and exposure are appealing, too. Client pressures and job burnout are among the negative aspects of the job.

The rewards, the pay, and the perks

The first 2 years in business are typically the most difficult, because huge amounts of money are invested in getting the store up and running. But after a clear profit surfaces by the third year, entrepreneurs can expect to stay in business—if they keep up with trends, maintain quality, and price their garments attractively. Fashion publicists earn a straight salary, with entry-level positions paying $21,000 annually. Full-time public relations specialists earn about $32,000, with top salaries at $70,000 per year.

Getting started

One of the best ways to get into the retail business is by working in it. Start by working as a sales-clerk at a clothing store in your neighborhood. Talk to other boutique owners and find out how they got started.

The public relations field requires strong writing and communication skills, so degrees in these areas are a must. Volunteer to help coordinate special events at your school as a way of gaining experience.

Climbing the career ladder

Here are some productive ways you can move your career along.

RETAIL

- Discover a new designer whose collection you can sell exclusively.
- Update your store's decor regularly.
- Do creative window displays.
- Invite fashion celebrities to your promotions.
- Attend many industry events and fashion shows.

PUBLIC RELATIONS

- Create a brilliant promotion.
- Network at parties and fashion shows.
- Work overtime.
- Keep in daily touch with the media.
- Practice public-speaking and presentation skills.

Now decide if a retail or promotional career in fashion is right for you

See if you share personality traits with some of the most successful store owners and publicists.

RETAIL

- Disciplined
- Risk taker
- Self-motivated
- Ahead of the times
- Dedicated
- Outgoing

PUBLIC RELATIONS

- Competitive
- Energetic
- Assertive
- Persistent
- Sharp
- Articulate

Things you can do to get a head start

Explore the following options to succeed as a fashion entrepreneur:

- Attend an art or design workshop.
- Apply for a salesclerk position.
- Read fashion trade publications.

If you're more inclined to promote the fashion industry, increase your knowledge by:

- Joining the staff of your school newspaper or literary magazine to hone your writing skills.
- Serving on the prom or home-coming committee to get a feel for special-event planning.
- Working part-time in a fashion-related occupation.
- Applying to a college that specializes in communications.

Let's Meet...

Jeffery Roberts and Nick Cave
Fashion Designers/Boutique Owners

Jeffery and Nick opened Robave, a women's high-fashion boutique, in 1993. They design their own high-quality clothes.

What first attracted you to a career in fashion design and retail?

NC: My foremost dream was to be an artist, which I truly am in my work as a designer. But I focused intensely on the fashion business following my years in college, where I majored in fibers and textiles. My areas of concentration were surface design, screenprinting, and painting on textiles. Our design studio and store have enabled us to broaden our fashion design scope to a larger audience.

Tell me how you got started in fashion design and retail.

JR: My background is in architecture and interior design. One day I was working on a furniture design project at an architectural firm, when I realized that I wanted to create things from my own design, not someone else's. Within 6 weeks, I sold my house and car, quit my job, and enrolled in a fine arts program. Those classes led me to fashion design and, ultimately, to co-owning a business.

Describe a typical day at work.

JR: Most days start at 8 A.M. and go until 11 P.M., at least 6 days a week. I spend a good portion of the day at the design studio, where I do flat patterns and help with constructing garments. The rest of my time is spent at the store, where I assist customers and get continuous feedback from them on the fit and style of our designs. Other tasks include accounting and bookkeeping, meeting with fabric representatives, sketching designs, and critiquing collections.

Describe one of your happiest moments on the job.

NC: The opening of the Robave store was one of the happiest moments of our life. It took about 3 years of planning and preparations, then it all came together for us.

What is the most difficult part of your job?

NC: As an artist, it's especially difficult dealing with the countless decisions that come with owning a business—such as accounting and legal issues.

Do you get to meet a lot of new people?

JR: Yes. I meet new people every week, and they're typically buyers, sales representatives, customers, employees, designers, and individuals who take tours of our studio.

Jeffery and Nick's Store Design

Because they approach fashion design from an artistic point of view, Jeffery and Nick put a great amount of effort into the interior design aspects of their store. Because it's enclosed by windows, it has a very open, spacious, bright mood. All the walls are white, as in an art gallery, so that the garments show up well.

The staff works together in one room so that the business becomes a visible team effort—each person has a purpose and interacts with the others. It's a very comfortable space. To promote creativity and put shoppers in a relaxed frame of mind, they play classical music.

Let's Meet...

Patrick Welsh
Fashion Public Relations Specialist

After working in retail sales, Patrick moved into the fast-paced arena of fashion public relations. He works for a major upscale U.S. department store and loves the variety, energy, and challenges of his job.

Did you need any special schooling or training for your work?

Yes. I hold a bachelor's degree in journalism and mass communications, which is what most companies require for public relations positions. I focused on honing both my oral and written communication skills to excel in this high-energy field.

Do you use the knowledge/skills you learned in school on the job?

I use my communication skills every day on the job. In public relations, communicating clearly and concisely is crucial. Whether I'm writing a press release or discussing a fashion promotion on a conference call, I rely on my oral and written expertise.

What do you like most about your work?

The most exciting aspect of my job is that it's constantly changing. No two days are ever the same. One day I may be planning a promotion for the following season, and the next day I may be conducting a special designer event. Each day brings a new set of challenges and triumphs.

Describe your work environment.

I work in an environment where everything moves very quickly. I constantly need to think on my feet, troubleshoot problems, and make critical decisions. Although it's exciting, it can also be stressful. So aspiring public relations specialists must learn how to manage their time and set daily goals.

Do you get to meet a lot of new people on the job?

I have the opportunity to meet and work with a lot of people from different areas, including the media, fashion studios, advertising, entertainment, and Fortune 500 companies.

Do you like to work alone or as part of a team?

I enjoy working on a team because it allows me to bring new and different perspectives to the table. I believe it helps make you more creative. You can bounce ideas off one another and receive honest feedback. It also allows you to learn from others how you can accomplish tasks more efficiently.

Patrick's Advice

Patrick has the following advice for students who want to break into fashion public relations:

- Apply for an internship with a department store, clothier, or public relations agency that has fashion accounts. You'll gain valuable experience and contacts in the industry.

- Perfect those oral and written communication skills by speaking in public, keeping a journal, and writing news and creative stories. This will make you an asset to any organization.

- Set up informational interviews with industry professionals to find out the successful career path they took.

- Read the trade publications to learn about the business the same way media industry leaders do. Don't read just *Vogue, Cosmopolitan,* or *Mirabella,* but also *Women's Wear Daily, W,* and *The Daily News Record.*

Success Stories

Coco Chanel Coco Chanel was a world-class designer whose upscale boutiques have a loyal following around the globe. In 1954, at the age of 71, she designed the classic "security suit," with gold buttons and braid trim. That look has set her stores apart from others for the past several decades. Karl Lagerfeld, another designer of legendary proportions, assumed management of the house of Chanel in 1983—further enhancing a billion-dollar design legacy.

Nicole Tysowsky Nicole Tysowsky is a merchandising representative for a top fashion publication. She's essentially a publicist, who has been in the business for 5 years and initially received most of her experience behind the scenes as a beauty editor. She produces a video twice a year that highlights the new seasonal wardrobe trends, and coordinates fashion shows and other exciting promotional events. Nicole literally lives out of a suitcase, traveling around the world speaking at major fashion extravaganzas to large groups of entrepreneurs, the media, and prospective customers.

Find Out More

You and the retail or promotional sides of fashion

For seeking a career in the retail or public relations fields, you need to get started by preparing the following important information and qualifications.

RETAIL

- Experience working with customers in any service-related job
- Ability to work with mathematical figures and percentages
- If you're also a designer, a sample collection and portfolio
- Artistic skills in display and interior design

PUBLIC RELATIONS

- Extensive portfolio of writing and promotional projects
- A sharp, concise, one-page resume
- Experience in special-event planning and media relations
- Public-speaking expertise

Find out more about careers in fashion retailing and promotions

These organizations can provide you with more information about retail and public relations careers in the fashion industry:

American Marketing Association
Philadelphia College of Textiles
    & Sciences
School of Business
Philadelphia, PA 19144

International Mass Retail
    Association
570 South Ave.
New York, NY 10018

National Retail Merchants
    Association
100 W. 31st St.
New York, NY 10001

Public Relations Society of
    America, Inc.
33 Irving Place
New York, NY 10003–2376

PR Reporter
P.O. Box 600
Exeter, NH 03833

FASHION
INSTRUCTOR

Many fashion-industry professionals want to pass on their knowledge to others. So they often work as instructors, teaching textiles or design. If you find yourself helping your fellow class-mates with assignments or feel very comfortable speaking in front of a group, consider teaching as a profession. Combine that with your talent for designing clothes and accessories or sketching, and you've got an ideal career. One that's flexible and rewarding.

What it's like to be a fashion instructor

The majority of design instructors are based in colleges and universities. They teach and advise more than 14 million full-time and part-time students in the United States. In specialized fashion institutes, a large number of teachers work part-time and divide their days between two schools. Their work combines lecturing with hands-on demonstration. Classrooms are more like workshops; students sketch garments, cut out patterns, and sew. It's up to the instructor to critique their creations, and give them constructive advice on improving their work and preparing for a productive career in fashion design.

Let's find out what happens on the job

As a fashion instructor, you'll spend much time preparing your lectures and class assignments. Because you are also a full-time designer or artist, you need to budget your workload so that you can devote complete attention to your various tasks. Say you teach two classes per day—one in the morning and one in the afternoon. Keep in mind that design schools offer intensive courses. One class typically lasts 3 hours and involves a lecture accompanied by visual aids, with the remaining 2 hours devoted to "manual labor," like drawing, cutting material, and draping it on a dress form. If your school day finishes around 4 P.M., you still have several hours to work on your own design projects. Other days include advising students, grading, and assisting with the school's fashion shows.

The pleasures and pressures of the job

One of the greatest rewards of being a fashion instructor is having a positive influence on an aspiring designer's career. You're nurturing young talent and preserving high standards within the fashion industry. You can also devise your own schedule, allowing you to do your own design work. Some of the less-enjoyable aspects of the job include having to dismiss or fail a problem student, long classroom hours, and deadline pressures.

The rewards, the pay, and the perks

Earnings for fashion instructors vary. Faculty in 4-year schools earn higher salaries, on the average, than those in 2-year schools. According to a recent survey by the American Association of University Professors, salaries for full-time faculty averages $43,000, with part-time instructors earning $27,700. Those figures drop slightly when applied to the fine arts profession, as opposed to law or business. A top perk is having summers off and long holiday breaks to attend to other fashion projects. You also have quick access to top fashion companies and professionals through your affiliation with a design school.

Getting started

In the fashion field, most faculty members are hired as instructors or part-time assistant professors. They typically hold a bachelor's or a master's degree in fine arts or textiles. Because fashion education centers offer courses from fabric design to drawing and merchandising, you want to find an area in which you excel. Then get experience in that particular field, supplement your education with community activities or fashion seminars, and start a portfolio of your best work.

Climbing the career ladder

- Join the executive committee of a local fashion association.

- Become computer literate.

- Teach additional fashion workshops and seminars.

- Publish a paper or book about the fashion industry.

- Work as a designer, retailer, or consultant.

Now decide if fashion teaching is right for you

Take the following quiz to see if you would pass with flying colors as a fashion instructor:

- Do you like to speak in front of large groups of people?

- Are you patient and attentive?

- Would you enjoy working in a school?

- Are you willing to spend long hours on the job?
- Does advising young designers appeal to you?
- Do you have a knack for encouraging others?
- Are you knowledgeable about fabrics and textiles?
- Do you also want to be a fashion designer or other specialist in the industry?

If you answered "yes" to these questions, then you've just received an "A" for your suitability for a career as a fashion instructor.

Things you can do to get a head start

Check out these pointers on getting your teaching career off to a good start:

- Take textile and public-speaking courses in high school.
- Apply for colleges that emphasize design and education.
- Volunteer to tutor students at your school.
- Help with organizing fundraising fashion shows for local groups and clubs.
- Work part-time in the fashion industry.
- Sharpen your writing and computer skills.

Let's Meet...

Denise M. Causher-Thompson
Fashion Instructor

Denise has been a fashion instructor for more than 10 years. She has studied design in London, coordinated the traveling "Ebony Fashion Fair," and operated her own clothing/accessories store.

Is a career as a fashion instructor something you always dreamed of?

I fell into it very naturally. As a child, I loved to design clothes for my paper dolls and in high school, I took a dressmaking course and continued to teach myself how to sew. When I was studying for my bachelor's degree in fashion design, I realized how much I loved helping other students with their projects.

Tell me how you got started in fashion education.

While I was working as a free-lance designer, I was asked to substitute for an illustration class at a local college. After that, I put together a resume and sent it to an area design school, and they hired me.

Describe a typical day on the job.

I work from a course outline and schedule that I've developed; it requires students to design and make their own garment in 3 weeks. We open class with a lecture and discussion about fabrics or marketing. Then I give a demonstration—of draping material, for example. Finally I oversee the students as they work on their individual projects. I make it a point to apply good examples of work and constructive criticism to the class as a whole so that my students can learn from each other.

What do you like most about your job?

- Interacting with students in a productive way.
- Helping students solve problems and giving them job leads.
- Taking my class on field trips to the apparel center, manufacturing facilities, and design studios.
- Instilling confidence in others.

What do you like least about your work?

- Having to say goodbye after a semester, because we've all become quite attached.
- Not being able to solve a tricky design problem immediately.
- Exhaustion from standing on my feet for many hours.
- Dealing with mechanical problems, like temperamental sewing machines.

Denise's Resume

When Denise M. Causher-Thompson applies for a fashion
teaching position, this is what her resume looks like.

Denise M. Causher-Thompson

ACADEMIC PREPARATION

School of the Art Institute of Chicago, Bachelor of Arts Degree,
Fashion Design, 1978.

Epsom College of Art and Design, London, Diploma, Fashion Design,
1976.

Northeast Surrey College of Technology, London, Diploma,
Management and Finance, 1976.

PROFESSIONAL BACKGROUND

Present | *INSTRUCTOR*, Ray College of Design, Chicago
International Academy of Merchandising & Design, Chicago
Cover all aspects of fashion patterns, draping, design, and
the business of fashion.

1989–1992 | *PATTERNMAKER*, Asoke Int. Taiwan, Chicago, Nigeria
Produced patterns for Womenswear Co. with manufacturing
in Europe, Asia, and Africa.

1989–1991 | *DESIGN CONSULTANT*, Sears, Montgomery Ward,
Chicago
Reported size and fit pattern and production changes.

1976–1988 | *FREELANCE DESIGNER & SPECIFICATION
TECHNICIAN* for the following companies: Barviani,
Chicago; Lady Barn, India; Vidal Sassoon, London; Myra
Everett, Chicago.
Duties included final production patterns and samples.

1980–1987 | *PRESIDENT*, Distinctive Artwear, Chicago
Owner and operator of small retail/wholesale manufacturing business, specializing in designer clothing and
accessories.

1977–1979 | *FASHION COORDINATOR/DISPLAY ARTIST*, The
Source, Chicago
Designed and arranged all displays in women's store.

1974–1976 | *WARDROBE COORDINATOR & SEAMSTRESS*, Ebony
Fashion Fair
Traveled throughout the U.S. coordinating the fashion line
for the show. After a successful tour, was promoted to position of Designer since 1976.

Let's Meet...

Veronica Chin
Fashion Instructor

For more than 10 years, Veronica has been teaching design students about the creative side of fashion—sketching, millinery, textiles, and its long history. She brings solid education and experience to the classroom.

Did you need any special schooling or training?

Yes. I received my bachelor of fine arts degree in fashion design, with a minor in theatrical costuming, and a master of science degree, which focused on extensive research, through my school's Environmental Textile Department. But experience is also crucial to an education position, and I worked in the garment industry for 6 years before beginning my teaching career.

What do you like most about your job?

Working with the students and seeing their creative development during a 3-year or 4-year period.

Do you use the knowledge/skills you learned in school on the job?

I use them every day. I still refer to my notes from lectures in college, as well as textile projects I worked on. Continuing education and ongoing research assignments are also important for college instructors if they want to be promoted and receive increases in pay.

What special skills do you need to be a good fashion instructor?

- Take communication and teach methodology courses.
- Consider a minor in education.
- Must have at least 6 years' experience in a specific fashion field, such as accessory design or sketching.

What do you like least about your job?

Grading, especially in an artistic profession like design, which tends to be very subjective. So it's a challenge for me to devise a point system that fairly charts a student's progress while allowing for constructive criticism and improvement. I also spend a great deal of time encouraging my students in class.

Is there a lot of competition for jobs in fashion instruction?

Yes, because there are not as many design schools as there are general academic institutions. Whenever you narrow your career to a specialized field, competition naturally increases.

Veronica's Ideal Classroom

Unlike a traditional academic environment, a design school's classrooms require more furniture than desks and blackboards. Veronica and her students do a lot of demonstration work and in-class projects. Her room resembles an artist's studio.

Here's Veronica's idea of the perfect design classroom:

- Very spacious, with plenty of room to work
- Large windows that filter in bright, natural light
- High-tech equipment, such as computerized sewing machines
- Wide pattern-cutting tables
- Dress forms of various shapes and sizes
- Hat blocks for millinery classes

Success Stories

Daniel Larson

Daniel Larson has a diverse plate of industry know-how to pass on to his students at the design school where he's been teaching for the past 14 years. Prior to teaching a wide range of fashion topics, he worked as a fashion coordinator, visual merchandising director, designer, and consultant. Since receiving his degree in fashion design, he's lived and breathed this fascinating business for nearly 40 years—and can't imagine being in any other field. His best advice to students is to keep an open mind and continue to learn even after they've graduated.

Marjorie E. Johnson

A fiber artist with a comfortable knack for teaching, Marjorie E. Johnson has been sharing her design expertise with students of all ages for almost 20 years. She conducts workshops that focus on creating wearable art. And her trademark style is a form of customized quilting done on jackets, vests, and shirts that features outdoor landscapes and animal prints. Marjorie encourages her students to find out, through trial and error, what aspect of fashion intrigues them the most—then "go for it, make it happen!"

Find Out More

You and fashion instruction

Here's some information that will help you start a "career file" for fashion teaching:

- Save your best classroom projects from high school.

- Keep outstanding reference letters from instructors and employers.

- Include your own personal sketches, patterns, and designs.

- Enter design competitions and stress awards you've won.

Find out more about becoming a fashion instructor

These organizations can provide you with more information about careers in fashion education:

American Association of
    University Professors
1012 14th St., N.W.
Washington, DC 20005

American Federation of Teachers
555 New Jersey Ave., N.W.
Washington, DC 20001

Fashion Group International
9 Rockefeller Plaza
New York, NY 10022

National Association of Schools of
    Art and Design
11250 Roger Bacon Dr.
Suite 21
Reston, VA 22090

FASHION JOURNALISTS AND PHOTOGRAPHERS

T wo of the most influential behind-the-scenes professions in fashion are journalism and photography. Imagine how empty the industry would be if there were no magazines filled with articles on the latest trends and bright, glossy photos of new styles! It would be pretty dreary. If you have a flare for the written word, or are handy with a camera shutter, fashion writing or photography may be an ideal career choice.

Both jobs are fast-paced and challenging, with opportunities to meet celebrities and travel.

What it's like to be a fashion journalist or photographer

Fashion journalists cover a wide range of topics, such as apparel, accessories, cosmetics, and fragrances. They work as copywriters; assistant, associate, and managing editors; editors/publishers; and freelance contributors. There's a highly-charged feel to this massive industry, where writers attend fashion shows around the world, interview famous designers and models, and report on colorful promotional events.

Fashion photography is very similar to journalism, with most photographers sending their pictures to magazines and newspapers. They work in the same lightning-paced environment and can also submit their film to garment catalogs and advertising agencies with fashion accounts.

Let's find out what happens on the job

Although fashion editors do a lot of writing, they also review submitted articles and plan the contents of their publication. Established writers may work on a freelance basis, selling their work to specific publications. Duties are generally split among covering events, writing about them, and meeting production deadlines. Proofreading and doing attractive page layouts come with the territory. Fashion photographers spend long hours setting up a photo shoot and working with models in a studio or on location, as well as developing their own photos.

The pleasures and pressures of the job

Fashion writers and photographers have ample opportunities to have their work read and viewed by millions of people. Photographers travel around the globe with models in tow.

On the flip side, they both work under enormous deadline pressure and often have to deal with temperamental personalities. Travel is quick and intense.

The rewards, the pay, and the perks

Salaries for fashion writers follow the same scale for journalists in other areas of specialization. Beginning salaries for writers and editorial assistants average $20,000 annually. Senior editors at the largest newspapers earn more than $60,000 a year. Perks include paid travel expenses, discounts on clothes and other fashion items, and much room for growth.

Full-time salaried photographers average about $22,000, with high salaries in the $50,000-a-year range. Many fashion photographers are self-employed, so their earnings fluctuate. Their biggest perks are travel and freedom to work outside the confines of an office.

Getting started

The best starting point for fashion journalism is a special writing seminar or workshop. Then find a college degree program that emphasizes journalism, communications, or English, with the option of minoring in fashion design or a related industry topic. For photographers, begin by subscribing to photography magazines. Look into classes with a fashion-related emphasis, and begin building a portfolio of your best work.

Climbing the career ladder

FASHION JOURNALIST

- Keep up-to-date on computer advancements.
- Stay overtime to meet your deadlines.
- Enhance your stories with unusual creative angles and styles.
- Belong to a prestigious journalism and fashion association.
- Come up with your own article ideas.

FASHION PHOTOGRAPHER

- Join a respected photography organization.
- Submit your pictures in photography competitions.
- Demonstrate your ability to work quickly and efficiently.

- Stay abreast of high-tech photography developments.
- Attend as many fashion events as possible.

Here are the qualities you need to succeed as a fashion writer:

Now decide if fashion writing or photography is right for you

- Hyper-organized
- Task oriented
- Works well under pressure
- Writes quickly and accurately
- Outstanding interviewing skills
- Curious

Here's a snapshot of the qualities of a winning fashion photographer:

- Technically oriented
- Creative/artistic
- High energy and stamina
- Self-motivated
- Confident
- Sharp, quick camera ability

Let's Meet...

Stacy Wallace-Albert
Fashion Editor and Publisher

Stacy's fashion magazine, *The A List*, highlights local designers and specialty stores. It features high-quality photo spreads and a contemporary layout, and has a large number of subscribers.

How did you get started in retail fashion publishing?

After moving to a new city, I spent a lot of time checking out the neighborhood boutiques. But I found no guide to direct me to these wonderful shops. So I decided to publish one, which involved matching a great opportunity with my willingness to take a risk.

Did you need any special schooling or training?

A substantial writing and production background is important. But I find that with owning a publication, my professional skills in sales and marketing have been critical to building a solid subscriber base.

What special skills do you need to be a good editor/publisher?

- Curiosity
- Enthusiasm
- Energy

- Organization
- Determination
- Confidence

What do you like most/least about your job?

The flexibility of my schedule allows me to be independent. The constantly changing market is always energizing, as are the endless opportunities for discovery and education. The main drawback, however, is the day-to-day administrative work that comes with running a business.

Describe your work environment.

Hectic! I work out of my home. So I have to take all my own telephone calls, solve editorial/production problems, and make decisions on the spot.

What do you see yourself doing 5 years from now?

I hope to own a larger communications company that includes more publications and a radio station. The focus would still be on fashion and lifestyle topics, because those are such forward-moving industries.

Articles in Stacy's Magazine

In addition to feature articles, Stacy's magazine is divided into "Fashion," "Home & Food," and "Departments" (Events Calendar, Resources, etc.) sections. Here's a sampling of some current subjects covered in *The A List:*

Let's Meet...

Sun Lee
Fashion Photographer

Sun Lee's photography career spans 23 years, with 11 spent chronicling fashion. He owns his own photography studio and is an expert in photographing models for national ad campaigns and catalogs.

What first attracted you to a career in fashion photography?

Actually my original career choice was to be an electrician, but I discovered how much I liked photography after taking pictures at a wedding that turned out very good. On my own, I continued to improve my technique and later got a job at a big advertising agency that specialized in product photography. That led to another photography job at an agency, which focused on fashion catalog work. The energy and creativity involved in designing appealing photo segments with professional models prompted me to continue working in this field.

Did you need any special schooling or training?

I'm essentially self-taught, but took some very helpful courses in dark room, black-and-white/color development, double exposure, lighting, and camera equipment. It's crucial for aspiring photographers to work as apprentices and

learn on the job. The best education is trial
and error.

What special skills do you need to be a good fashion photographer?

You have to acquire an artist's eye and per-
ception. You must have a working knowledge
of math and science because your equipment
is so technical. For example, in order to do a
meter reading, you need to program the
right series of numbers to balance the lighting. You should also become well-versed in
computers, especially with filmless cameras
that are programmed by a compact disk.

What do you like most/least about your job?

I love clicking the shutter, knowing that I'm
creating exciting visual work. Photo shoots
are exhilarating and inspiring for me. In
fashion, one of the biggest frustrations is
dealing with late models.

What advice would you give young people starting out in fashion photography?

Always walk around with a camera because
you never know when a perfect photo opportunity will arise. By making your camera a
part of you, a sense of comfort and familiar-
ity is achieved. Practice as much as you can.
Join a photography club or take some specialized courses. Taking photos for your
school's yearbook or newspaper are excellent
starting points.

On a Photo Shoot with Sun Lee

Let's join Sun Lee during a long day of photographing models for a fashion catalog.

8 A.M.   Study transparencies of film shot yesterday. Select best photos for client.

8:30 A.M.   Prepare studio for photo session.

9 A.M.   First wave of models starts arriving. Work with a stylist and an assistant, who set up props and adjust the models' clothes and makeup. Spend about 30 minutes per model groupings.

Noon   Break for a quick lunch and send out film to be developed. Expect to photograph about 25 models today.

1 P.M.   Devise new combinations and situations for models that show the clothes at their best. Work until 6 p.m. with no break.

6 P.M.   Meet with client to discuss the day's sessions. Send out second batch of film.

7 P.M.   Break for dinner.

8 P.M.   Continue photographing more models for 2 hours.

10 P.M.   Take this time to review the day's work and plan for the next series of photo sessions.

Success Stories

Virginia Pope As the fashion editor of the *New York Times* from 1933 to 1955, Virginia Pope brought fashion writing to a highly respected level. Known as the "Dean of Fashion Editors," she was a pioneer in transmitting photos by wire of Paris openings to New York for the next day's editions. She was also the first editor to take readers into New York's prestigious Seventh Avenue showrooms. But the venerable Miss Pope is probably best known for championing the emerging American ready-to-wear designers.

Allan Murray Fashion photographer Allan Murray started his career many years ago in front of the camera as a model and television commercial actor. Today, he specializes in photographing model composites and portfolios, as well as on-location sessions. Allan is unique among his peers because he's entirely self-taught, having spent a long time getting tips from photographers, including the famed Victor Skrebneski, with whom he worked. His captivating black-and-white fashion photography work is in great demand within the modeling industry and advertising agencies specializing in fashion.

Find Out More

You and fashion journalism or photography

Here are a few questions you should be able to answer to get off to a strong start in fashion journalism or photography.

FASHION JOURNALISM

- What degrees are required for a fashion writing position?
- At what level will you most likely start out in a magazine or newspaper office?
- What types of stories get covered in fashion publications?

FASHION PHOTOGRAPHY

- What kinds of skills does fashion photography require?
- List three fashion photography situations.
- What are the main tools of your trade besides a camera?

Find out more about becoming a fashion writer or photographer

For further information about the fashion journalism and photography professions, contact these organizations:

FASHION WRITER

American Society of Magazine
  Editors
575 Lexington Ave.
New York, NY 10022

Fashion Group International
9 Rockefeller Plaza
New York, NY 10022

The Newspaper Guild
8611 Second Ave.
Silver Spring, MD 20912

FASHION PHOTOGRAPHER

American Society of Media
  Photographers
Suite 502–14
Washington Road
Princeton Junction, NJ 08550

National Press Photo Association
3200 Croasdaile Dr.
Durham, NC 27705

Professional Photographers of
  America
1090 Executive Way
Des Plaines, IL 60018

INDEX

85